WE ARE MORE THAN
CONQUERORS

*Fervent ladies witnessing God ordering their steps through
their testimonial experiences.*

JANET G. SNIPE

Printed in the United States of America
First Printing, 2021
ISBN: 978-0-578-87621-4

Published by DoQuoi Green Ministries
4780 Ashford Dunwoody Rd. Suite A #199
Atlanta, GA 30338
www.doquoigreen.org

Dedication

This book is dedicated in memory of my mother Thelma Louise Green who taught me to persevere. She prepared me for life's challenges which enables me to face them with love. She was the inspiration and encourager who gave me the strength to be great in everything, and to achieve my goals in life.

To my grandchildren London, D'Laysia, Alathia, and to all of my future grandchildren, I love each of you to infinity and beyond forever and forever.

First Lady Janet G. Snipe
"We Are More Than Conquerors"

Table of Contents

Acknowledgments

First, I thank God most of all for giving me this vision because without God I wouldn't be able to do any of this.

To my husband, Rev. William Snipe, thank you for your unconditional love, prayers and support. To my son, Apostle DoQuoi (Pastor Donna) thank you both for your leadership and excellent teaching on bringing God's kingdom on earth and spiritual warfare. To my daughter and best friend D'Leta (Dezmond), thank you all for your prayers, love, support, and always being there for me. Thank you all for blessing William and me with beautiful grandchildren. To my siblings, family, and friends, thank you all for your continuous support.

To each of my resilient authors, the fervent ladies who fearlessly shared their stories to encourage and inspire others; I thank God for ordaining you to be a part of this vision. Keep God first as we continue to advance by bringing His glory and kingdom on earth.

To DoQuoi Green Ministries, thank you for your professional guidance in publishing this project.

To my brother-in-law Roy (Karen) Snipe, thank you for the beautiful design of this book.

Thank you to everyone who will read this book. Know that you are no longer a survivor; you have overcome and are more than a conqueror.

Foreword

There can be no debate as to the fact that we are all products of our environment. Our personalities, goals, and desires are shaped by the situations, circumstances, and places we encounter on this journey called life. God's most dedicated and committed people have been prompted by life events to ask, "Why?" Before hearing the Spirit, the flesh proceeds to question God. It questions why something is happening or has happened. When we initially encounter a test, we rarely recognize it as a testimony.

Through the inspiration of God, First Lady Janet G. Snipe has encouraged women to share their "Why?" moments with others as she was made to realize that we all have a story. No matter how insignificant we deem it to be, God can use it as the answer to someone else's "Why?" All of the accounts contained herein may not be for you, but all are for someone. God is using all who contributed to this book to help others find their way. In 1 Samuel 30:11, He put an Egyptian in place to show David the way. After this encounter,

David went on to defeat the enemy who had taken everyone and everything that he held dear. With the help of a man thought to be worthless and left in a field to die, David recovered all that he lost and more.

Now He has put these women in place to give guidance to others on their journeys. They have become God's instruments to strengthen the weak, guide the lost, and lift up the downtrodden. Their stories attest to the fact that we are more than conquerors (Romans 8:37). The God we serve will always give us what we need to overcome our adversities. I implore you to take advantage of this tool that God has given to aid you in life's travels. These women themselves are more than conquerors, not by their own might but through God's love for them. Because of His love for you, God has allowed them to produce this book. It will prepare some readers for what they will have to go through. It will minister to some as they go through. Lastly, it will give comfort to those who've been through.

Never forget that God's Word is living and true. It speaks to our individual needs, situations, and conditions. It is through these various authors that His Word is manifested. It is through His divine wisdom that this book was written. With His blessing, it is made available to you. It is confirmation that you all are more than conquerors.

Rev. William Snipe
Pastor/Servant
African Methodist Episcopal Church

Obedience is Better than Sacrifice

First Lady Janet G. Snipe

Every weekend, a group of my lady friends and I would gather to hang out and enjoy one another's company. Everyone would bring something to contribute in celebration of another work week well done. We would sit around and relax, make jokes, listen to music, and all around have a good time. These moments brought back so many good memories to me and the ladies.

On one very special day, I had a vision that was sent to me from God Himself. He showed me how strong my social skills were and how I could use that trait to carry out His will! He showed me a specific book. I immediately obeyed God's command and purchased that book. I read an amazing book by Priscilla Shirer, *Fervent: A Woman's Battle Plan to Serious, Specific and Strategic Prayer.* This book inspired the name of my women's group, Fervent Ladies. Fervent Ladies was the vision given to me as a confirmation of the need for prayer all around. According to crosswalk.com, "Fervent prayer is a deep, focused, and passion-filled petition to God." The purpose of this group is to empower one another, seek God, and make prayer a lifestyle. I shared the vision with my husband, William, and he thought it was a great idea.

In 2016, while attending my sister's birthday celebration, while my friends and family were gathered and enjoying themselves, I figured this would be the perfect time to share with them my instructions from the Lord. I explained to the ladies what God wanted me to do, and they all were enthused with the idea. So, in preparation for what God had next, we all agreed to read the book by Priscilla Shirer. We decided to meet at the end of the month at my home to discuss the book in detail. This reminded me of God's instruction to take His Word to the world, "*And he said unto them, Go ye into all the world, and preach the gospel to every creature*" (Mark 16:15 KJV).

The first meeting was held on a Saturday at 10 in the morning. I was so excited but also so nervous. The doorbell rang, and to my surprise, only five of the fifteen ladies invited showed up. I was so disappointed because many had expressed an interest in attending. Nevertheless, I did not allow that to stop me from being obedient to the instructions from God. As I opened in prayer, God reminded me about Matthew 18:20 (KJV), *"For where two or three are gathered together in my name, there am I in the midst of them."*

The enemy will always try to test whatever God assigns you to do. He tried to shut me down and have me give up by having me see through my natural eyes, but because of God's glory, I walk by faith and not by sight. As time went on, I continued to be obedient and faithful. The group started to expand as more women joined. God revealed to me that some of the people I thought were my friends were not ready to go on this journey. When God gives you a vision or warns you about someone, you need to take heed of it and be obedient to the instructions He gives.

I was able to conquer what the naysayers, doubters, and the enemy tried to plant in my mind. By being a servant leader, praying to God, staying focused on the assignment at hand, trusting God through it all, keeping the faith no matter what, and obeying God's command, I had the confidence to step out on faith and follow my dreams and visions. No matter how big or small the assignment is, it is important to follow the Word of God and be obedient to the assignments given. God blesses and rewards obedience.

Once I started spending more time and having an intimate relationship with Jesus, I gained more understanding of who I am in Christ Jesus. I overcame the burdens and bondage of trying to please everyone and from being moved by what I see in the natural. I know the importance of obeying God no matter what because He is trusting me to manage His vision. I have surrendered my will to the Lord as He has instructed in His Word: *"Now if you will obey me and keep my covenant, you will be my own special treasure from among all the peoples on earth; for all the earth belongs to me"* (Exodus 19:5 NLT).

In conclusion, I leave you with this. You can conquer whatever obstacles you may encounter and rest in the confidence that if you know it's God's vision, He will bring all the pieces together as you stay in obedience to Him. You are never in it alone. God always sends what you need for His vision that He placed in you.

They Call Me Crazy

Cassandra Middleton Minson

Ever since I was a little girl, I can remember sitting in my grandmother's living room playing on her black, antique upright piano. Whenever I went to my grandmother's house, I would spend most of my visit making what I thought was a joyful noise while banging the keys on her piano. Lo and behold, I went there one day and the piano was gone! My grandmother had sold it. I was heartbroken that my noisy play date had abandoned me for a new home. My grandmother felt my sorrow and comforted me by allowing me to make noise on the church piano before going home every Sunday after church.

My mom had an intuition that I had a passion for music and asked me one day if I was interested in taking music lessons. I immediately jumped with joy and said yes! My mom went and bought a piano before finding me a music teacher. I guess it showed how much confidence she had in me.

In 1966, when I was 10 years old, I took piano lessons from an awesome music teacher that my mom found. She lived in downtown Charleston, South Carolina. My music teacher was very stern, and during that time, I thought she was very mean. Later, I realized she wanted the best for me and wanted me to be a great musician.

I can remember like yesterday how I would practice sometimes during the day and night. The piano was in the living room, which was the coldest part of the house. So cold that I could see the breath coming from my mouth because my mom would cut off the electric heater in the room before going to bed. She would say, "You better go to bed," but I would still go back in the living room to get on the piano. My siblings would say, "Oh my gosh, she is banging again!"

Before going to music school, I always wanted to get an A+ on whatever music composition I played, so I would play it to perfection. My music teacher was tough and would not settle for anything less. Playing my first hymn was very exciting to me. My mom was in the choir and she would sing along with me until I got the song right. She was always there to give me encouragement when others would criticize me.

I learned how to play within two years. At age 12, I started playing for the Sunday school at my church. My salary wasn't much, yet it was plenty of money for a 12-year-old, especially during the year 1968. When I wasn't knowledgeable about playing a certain song, I would ask for help as needed. I started playing as a full-time musician in my early years of high school. I rejected many jobs that required me to work on Sundays because of my commitment to my church.

After learning the basic techniques of music, I wanted to learn how to play by ear. I didn't know that it had to be a gift from God. I prayed without ceasing, though nothing seemed to change. I had an aunt who was an evangelist, and she said if you ask God for something, make sure that you are sincere about it. She also said that all things are possible if you only believe.

My aunt always carried a bottle of "blessing oil" (anointing oil to the politically correct) with her. She anointed my fingers, and I remember holding up my hands and the tears were flowing from my eyes. My aunt said to focus on Jesus and tell Him what you want with a sincere heart and He will shower you with His blessings. It didn't happen instantly, but I went to church one Sunday, and someone started singing a song. I hesitated to play at first, but when I touched those keys, God used me, and ever since then, I have been playing by ear. I am a true believer that God may not come when we want Him, but He is always on time.

My mom's denomination was Pentecostal Holiness, and after learning how to play by ear, I would go and play at her church. My fingers got a great workout whenever I played at my mother's church because each song would take about fifteen minutes before ending. It didn't matter to me because God gave me what I asked for by anointing my fingers. He gave me that blessing, and I wasn't tired of using it.

In 1975, I went to college but still would come home on weekends to play. Many opportunities to play for different churches were offered to me in the city where I attended college, yet I was content building the music ministry at my church. I played for weddings, afternoon services, and funerals without being compensated, especially for people who had done favors for me.

I believe in the saying that says, "Hand come, and hand go," meaning if someone gives you something with a sincere heart, you should be able to give them something in return. My children would say that I like to reminisce about what people have done for me by saying, "I remember when Betty Lou used to change your Pampers when y'all were babies, so I am not going to charge nothing for playing for her." They would laugh and I would tell them that God will provide, and He will continue to do great things for me.

There's a song by the Refuge Temple Deliverance Choir called "Fully Committed," and I feel that making the sacrifice to do what God wants and asks of me will pay off one day. Yes, they call me crazy, but guess what? They don't know my story. Playing for my church was always my priority and that was what I committed myself to do for more than forty years. Psalm 37:5 (NASB) says, *"Commit your way to the LORD, / Trust also in Him, and He will do it."* Even after graduating from college, I was still committed to my church.

In 2001, our church moved into a new sanctuary not knowing how we were going to pay for it because many people who voted to have the church built left us in a mortgage debt. The church's deficit caused my salary to decrease tremendously, but I still committed myself to stay anyway. Proverbs 16:3 (NASB) says, *"Commit your works to the LORD / And your plans will be established."* I know that because of my commitment, God has given me so many blessings.

I still don't know why God has not moved me yet. I ask God, "Why am I still here?" I know that I should not question Him, but I do. "They Call Me Crazy" by Norris Turner says: "They call me crazy ever since my savior took control." God is in control, and how crazy can you get praising Him and only Him? Nothing is better than getting crazy for the Lord because He is our all and all.

I had a grand-aunt who died in 2016. She was 107 years old and was the sexton of our church for numerous years. She would go every Saturday morning to clean our church. During that time, I didn't have a key to the church so I would get up early and go with her just to play the organ. I didn't take organ lessons, but through God's grace, I acquired the knowledge to learn on my own. I stayed at the church from the time my grand-aunt started cleaning until she was finished. We were like Alpha and Omega. She would vacuum and hum while I'd play a common meter hymn and encourage her in island dialect, "Gon Gal, you sound good!"

It is 2019 as I write, and I am still holding on. My salary has not been restored as of this day, but that is alright because my blessings are still flowing. Some people are still calling me crazy because I am probably the lowest paid musician in town. Others boast that God has a special place for me in heaven. "Heaven Belongs to You" by the Alabama Gurlz says, "If you live, pray, and sing right heaven belongs to you." I feel that heaven will belong to me not only because of my playing but the life that I live. I am praying for the Lord to continue to anoint my fingers and give me strength so I can be more devoted and committed to Him and my church. First Kings 8:61 (NASB) says, *"Let your heart therefore be wholly devoted to the LORD our God, to walk in His statutes and to keep his commandments, as at this day."*

Finally, I encourage you to:

1. Stay committed to whatever you are passionate about doing. Seek the Lord with all your heart, and He will bless you abundantly. Be obedient to His Word, and He will give you the ability to conquer any obstacles in your way. Commit to His Word and commit to His will.

2. Trust God at all times because He's always there for us. *"Trust in the LORD forever, / for the LORD GOD is an everlasting rock"* (Isaiah 26:4 ESV). Get rid of doubts and fear by trusting in the Lord with all your heart, mind, and soul.

3. Being determined gives you the insight to keep going despite the roadblocks. When we are determined about doing, remember that God is always on our side and He will never leave us. TO GOD BE THE GLORY!!!

They Call Me Crazy

People call me crazy
because they don't understand.
My work is for the Lord.
It is certainly not for man!
The craziest thing about it,
what people fail to see—
God's got his eyes on the sparrow
and I know he is watching me!
He is watching when I don't get paid
and he is watching when I do.
You can call me crazy
because your foot is not in my shoe.
Yes, they call me crazy
because many times my services are free.
It will be alright one day
because heaven has a special place for me.

-Cassandra Middleton Minson

It Wasn't an Accident

D'Leta Snipe-Waring

Don't you just love when you have finally made it through what felt like such a long, exhausting week and Friday finally comes? It seemed like you had been waiting forever for the weekend to get here. You even find yourself in such a good mood knowing that you can soon go home, wind down, and prepare yourself for an eventful or relaxing weekend. Like most do, we find ourselves listening to music while driving in our cars. I personally prefer listening to gospel music. I am not sure about anyone else, but I listen and vibe to gospel music just like anyone else would to any other genre.

Over the years, I have come to the realization that I enjoy having intimate time with the Lord in my car. My car is like my safe place, where I find myself being able to praise and worship God. I get to have some intimate, one on one time with Him. I can be a little free from everything and solely focus on Him spiritually (and physically on the road, of course).

As believers in the Lord Jesus Christ, we must develop an intimate relationship with our Father. A time where we can dwell in His presence and simply seek His face and thank Him for sacrificing His son Jesus. Luke 5:16 (NIV) says, *"But Jesus often withdrew to lonely places and prayed."* Having an intimate relationship with Him means we are not just asking for our needs and wants, but we go and sit at the throne of our Father and get into His Word, listening for His voice and instructions for our lives. I believe in the Scripture Matthew 6:33 that says if we seek Him and put Him first, there will be no need or desire to ask Him for anything because seeking Him alone will add all those other things. He will answer prayers you never even prayed.

On Friday, April 6, 2018, I was headed for the door at 11:45 p.m.; my weekend had officially started. I was approximately fifteen minutes away from the job and fifteen minutes away from home when I thought to myself, "It sure feels like I need a wheel alignment done." At the time, I was riding with two used tires (being cheap) that were put on my car the previous week after hitting a pothole that blew out both back tires.

Per usual, I was grooving to some gospel music on Heaven 100.1 at about a couple of minutes after midnight, making it Saturday, April 7. Suddenly, I heard a noise and felt a jerk. I automatically knew right then it had to have been at least one of my rear tires. I immediately tried to slow down all while being in the left lane and holding on to the steering wheel with my eyes wide open. The only thing I could think of at that given time was to repeatedly call on the name of Jesus. My car hit the left barrier, and before I knew it, the car had spun a couple of times in the middle of the four-lane interstate. I was not scared at all; I just knew what name to call on.

When the car came to a stop, I was back on the left shoulder of the interstate. I glanced down at the radio, and to my surprise, it was still playing like nothing had ever occurred. Then there was a knock on my window with a random guy asking if I was ok. I smiled and replied, "Yes, I'm fine. I just had to keep calling on the name of Jesus, and I'm glad to be alive."

After he left from the window, in a hurry, I started to look for my glasses that had flown off my face. To my surprise, I found them in one piece. Lord knows I don't know what I would have done if they were broken. Once I found my glasses, I went ahead and took out my license, registration, and insurance information so that I could be prepared for the police. In addition, I needed to get out of the car for safety reasons. I made my way out of the car to see the back bumper up against the cement barrier and the front end of the car in the left lane at a slant. The trunk was smashed in with the rubber tires completely off the rims. The back window had shattered, filling the back seat with glass, and the front lights were smashed. My car of almost ten years was done for.

The EMS came, along with the fire trucks, blocking off the left lane to ensure other cars would not hit us. One of the EMTs asked if they could evaluate me. I asked, "Do you have to?" And she replied, "No." I thought to myself, "I am not going in the back of anyone's ambulance for them to charge me when I feel just fine."

While on the scene, I noticed that one of the firefighters worked at the guard's gate at my job. Seeing a familiar face made me feel better about everything. He brought to my attention that I was blessed to be unharmed with it being late at night and the start of the weekend when many people, sober and drunk, are on the roadways. The place where my car spun around was right at the start of barriers splitting the lanes on the right near the exit. If the barriers were not there, my car could have gone across all the other lanes, putting me at a higher risk of being hit by the oncoming traffic or going off into the ditch, possibly hitting a tree or two.

I can say that I am truly blessed to have been in that situation where no other motorists were involved, nor did I have any major scratches or bruises. Prior to me leaving work that night, I was on Facebook and just so happened to see an extremely horrible accident appear on my newsfeed that involved a couple whose car ended up being smashed under an eighteen-wheeler. They both testified how good God had been and that they were not believers until that day. I remember looking in amazement at how they were not badly hurt under the horrific conditions of the accident. So many thoughts ran through my mind.

The next day, it came to me. Close to the end of March, I had posted a Facebook status that said, "I'm so fed up with the enemy and I'm tired of him using people! I'm just so tired but NOT tired of fighting back! The devil and his crew want to have their hands in everything! But, 'I Declare War.' #IDeclareWar!!!"

I knew right then that the enemy had tried to take me out. It was no "accident" but a strategically planned attack pretty much saying "game on." But I declared war with my wicked enemies when I put my foot down and made that Facebook status. The enemy was so strategic in his attempt that he did not involve anyone else and chose a time where no one would be riding with me. I thank God for His guardian angels that were there with me, protecting me from the plan of the enemy.

One month later, I had the pleasure of purchasing my first car the day after Mother's Day. I was blessed enough to not only get a new car but to get the car that I had always wanted. Everything was going so great regardless of the unfortunate event the month before. God saw what the enemy had planned for my downfall. So He interceded and the enemy's plan was halted once again. He did not let the enemy touch me because He had the ultimate plan.

In May 2018, I also found out that I was pregnant. I was so overjoyed! On February 7, 2019, God allowed me to give birth to a beautiful baby girl, making my husband and me first-time parents. In 2018, the month of April brought on an unfortunate event, but by God's grace, the month of May brought so much excitement and joy.

Fast forward to the month of June 2020. My husband and one-year-old witnessed a car in front of us go across a median into oncoming traffic, causing a multiple-car accident. The next week, I saw another accident that had taken place moments before I got to a stoplight on my way to work. I then could feel the Holy Spirit telling me that the enemy was up to something again. I made sure I stayed in prayer, asking God to continue protecting me and my family from the seen and unseen on the highways and byways. A week later, my daughter and I left my parents' house to head home. Before leaving their driveway, my mom said a quick prayer for us declaring we were covered by the blood of Jesus. We left the driveway, and I decided to pick back up on her prayer myself.

After leaving the neighborhood, my daughter and I got to a red light just before our turn and BAM! Here I was sitting at the light in prayer, and someone just hit me and my daughter from the rear. Immediately, the car's airbags deployed, and I banged my hand on the steering wheel in disbelief at what just happened. At that moment, my phone rang, but I had no idea where it was and my glasses were no longer even on my face to find it. Thankfully, I had my phone connected to the car's Bluetooth, and there, I saw my husband's number appear on the screen. I was able to answer and inform him about the accident. I then started praying loudly and earnestly, which then turned into a panic remembering that my child was in the back seat asleep.

I yelled, "My baby, my baby," and a young guy came to my passenger door asking, "Ma'am, are you okay?" All I could do was point to the back seat and say, "Yes, get my baby." I took my seatbelt off and tried to get out quickly, but the door wouldn't open, so I turned to the right and the guy who was at the door was trying to put his mask on to prevent spreading the COVID-19 virus. At that moment, I couldn't wait for him to put his mask on as a safety precaution. I just knew I had to get to my child, so I jumped over the console and got out of the car, struggling to open the back door. I kept on praying and managed to get her out of her damaged car seat. I was in disbelief at how fast things just took a turn. We were literally two minutes away from my parents' house and seconds away from the turn that would get us off that highway.

There I was again, witnessing the third multiple-car "accident" that month, with this particular one involving not just me but our daughter as well as four other families. Looking at my car and the others, mine was in the worst condition. My car was totaled, but without question, God totally had His hands on us. My daughter and I were able to walk away from the scene without any major damages!

Hours later, I was informed that my father saw a snake while out in the backyard. Thankfully, he saw it and managed to kill it, later realizing that it was a copperhead. When I heard the news, I just thought about how often my parents and daughter are in the backyard. It again let me see a strategy of the enemy. It was a strategic attack on me and my family. Had we not left my parents' house when we did, we too could've had an encounter with that snake.

I am a living witness of how God took what the enemy meant for evil and used it for my good (Genesis 50:20). I am so thankful for having God on my side, sparing me and my family's lives. All praises and honor belong to the Most High God for His continuous grace and mercy. In addition, He gave me the power and authority to fight back and take charge over my life. Through my circumstance, I not only had to take it to God in prayer, but I had to fight and wage war.

Spiritual warfare is a fight, battles between the kingdom of God and the kingdom of Satan, which is the kingdom of light versus the kingdom of darkness. First Peter 5:8 (NKJV) says that Satan is our adversary and goes around *"like a roaring lion, seeking whom he may devour."* Satan wants to devour the children of God. We must use the power and authority that God has given and fight back in the spirit, not physically. But as Ephesians 6:12 (NKJV) says, *"For we do not wrestle against flesh and blood but against principalities, against powers, against the rulers of the darkness of this age, against spiritual hosts of wickedness in the heavenly places."* It rightfully is my duty as a child of God to rule and reign here on Earth, and I must take back the territory in my life that belongs to God.

The enemy wants to try and stop everything pertaining to God, like our marriage, family, dreams, goals, finances, etc. Knowing that the enemy is here on his job, trying to cause us harm and even trying to kill us, we have no choice but to grab our weapons of power and fight back in the spirit. Let us take a stand and fight back for what God has ordained us to have. God may allow you to go through some things just so that in the end, when He brings you out, He can get all the glory He deserves. He never leaves us even when we are going through different situations and can't see the end of the tunnel.

We as the body of Christ must learn that most things we encounter are more spiritual than physical. We must not look at the day to day things in a fleshy, physical way, but spiritually. The enemy is no match for God, and their power isn't greater than the Lord's. The enemy will have you thinking that it was an "accident" when it was their plan all along. When an obstacle comes your way, just know that something greater is going to come out of it. Stay focused on the Word of God. When things don't look to be going in a positive direction, know that the Lord will work it out and turn it around.

In the end, I won the battle. I declared war with the enemy and took home the trophy. Wherever you are in your life, you too can win the battle, but you must become more than a conqueror in Christ Jesus, by accepting Him into your life. You can accept Christ in your life by repeating Romans 10:9-10 (NIV) which says, *"If you declare with your mouth, 'Jesus is Lord,' and believe in your heart that God raised Him from the dead, you will be saved. For it is with your heart that you believe and are justified, and it is with your mouth that you profess your faith and are saved."* I am forever grateful to be His child, and knowing that I am more than a conqueror gives me the power to conquer anything that comes my way.

A Faith Walk: The Ups and Downs

Dr. Lakeleia Middleton Robinson

Most of us hear people quote the phrase "walk by faith and not by sight" so freely, and we think, "Hey! I'm going to try that." Paul tells us that faith *"is the substance of things hoped for, the evidence of things not seen"* (Hebrews 11:1 KJV). Abraham was a man of faith who obeyed when he was called to go out and went out not knowing where he was going. Let me warn you, living by faith is not an easy lifestyle. Walking by faith requires determination, courage, strength, and trusting God in every circumstance. When you think about faith, you must think about the good and the rough times.

I had grown up and lived in South Carolina my entire life, which made the transitioning process difficult as we considered relocating. My emotions and feelings were everywhere because I believe "home is where the heart is." Most of all, life was comfortable! God had blessed me with a beautiful and healthy family, gainful employment with a government agency, a teaching position at a local university, a nice home in a wonderful community, and so many other wonderful opportunities and cherished moments. Yes, life was good! But ultimately, there is a moment in life when a decision must be made when we do not understand all the crucial factors.

One day, my husband smiled and said, "How do you feel about relocating?" I looked at him and replied, "I feel as though we are already established here, and our son is about to begin high school." He said God had spoken to him in more than one way about us relocating. This got my attention. I questioned my husband about if he heard God correctly or confirmed it was God's voice.

After a couple of days of meditating and pondering, other questions were, "Should I relocate or stay? God, do you really want me to leave my government job that I personally asked you for, sell our house, and leave everything behind? THIS IS JUST CRAZY!" At that moment, a Scripture appeared to me, 1 Corinthians 11:3: *"But I want you to know that the head of every man is Christ, the head of woman* is *man, and the head of Christ is God"* (NKJV). I said, "Lord, this just scares me, but it is going to take a leap of faith. If it is your will, you will bring forth confirmation."

This was going to test our faith and marriage. Eventually, the house was placed on the market for sale on a Monday evening, and on Wednesday morning an offer was made. In addition to that, the buyers offered a higher price. This sounds crazy, but was this our confirmation? And eventually, because of our faith in the Lord, we arrived and settled in Raleigh, North Carolina, one month later.

After weeks of intense unpacking, the devil was trying to steal my joy. I was experiencing the fear of the unknown; unwillingness to part with family, church family, and friends; and anxiety over change. Satan was trying to intimidate me with lies, pressure, and deception. I had to let Satan know he had no place, power, or authority over me.

This began a whirlwind of testing our faith and marriage. My husband and I were both without employment and operating solely off savings and net proceeds of home sales. Our eldest son was entering high school and the youngest was in elementary. The schools they were zoned in were not the most desirable schools for educating your children. So my husband suggested the idea of private school. I said once again, "Lord, this just scares me. Where will the funds come from to place our kids in a private school setting? THIS IS JUST CRAZY!" I was reminded of Matthew 14:31 (NKJV), *"'O you of little faith, why did you doubt?'"* I said, "This is indeed a fearful leap of faith, but I will trust you, Lord."

However, there was quite a shift in our spiritual walk. We visited an influx of churches to create a connection within the body of Christ. I felt overwhelmed, depressed, and concerned that my husband did not recognize the voice of God. I realized that during a crisis, the greatest threat to your faith is having a negative mind-set. This can give Satan an entry point to attack and defeat.

Fast forward about five months later: it felt as if we were beginning to sink into a financial crisis. In the meantime, my husband, a licensed master barber, was offered an opportunity at a local barbershop as a new barber in the area. But the daily income did not meet the standards of living.

We prayed daily for a breakthrough. I felt like we were getting nowhere; disappointment, discouragement, and doubt tried to creep in almost daily. I would feel stressed, depressed, and emotionally weighed down. I was hurting behind my smile. The enemy was trying to attack my family, body, and mind.

Weeks later, I had a dream. In this dream, a lady dressed in white embraced me and quoted Jeremiah 29:11: *"For I know the thoughts that I think toward you, says the LORD, thoughts of peace and not of evil, to give you a future and a hope"* (NKJV). I was reassured that this late-night encounter with God helped me refocus my faith, and I could trust He knew and heard my call for help.

After my seven months of unemployment, I secured a position with a biotech pharmaceutical company that offered work from home opportunities and generous benefits packages. We continued to meditate and stand on God's Word. I uttered daily, "Lord, you brought us too far to leave us now."

Near the one-year mark of unemployment, my husband secured a position with a market-leading logistics company, where he uses his customer service and managerial skills. In addition to this blessing, I was offered an adjunct faculty position teaching online courses in my field of study. My children have successfully completed two terms in their new school. And though we are not connected to a church body in our new home, that has not hindered our progress.

Despite our issues, we have had to learn to embrace what is in front of us and let go of what was behind us. MOVE FORWARD! If you choose this path, you must be willing to get out of your comfort zone. You will be misunderstood, called foolish, and feel abandoned. He is teaching you to trust Him so He can do something exceedingly, abundantly better than you've ever dreamed possible (Ephesians 3:20-21). He is teaching you to let go and trust Him with your heart and your soul, and He will direct your path (Proverbs 3:5-6).

Some powerful life lessons I have learned from this faith walk are:

1. Be able to recognize God during the storm.
2. *"Trust in the Lord with all your heart, / And lean not on your own understanding"* (Proverbs 3:5 NKJV).
3. Being a Christian is not just a title; it is a calling.
4. We go through storms so that God can perfect us.
5. We are more than a conqueror; our faith is long.
6. Faith must be in the right perspective.
7. Nothing is too hard for God. You've just got to trust the process.
8. Despite how we may feel about our circumstance, it proclaims that we are victorious.

Redirecting My Direction

Tameka C. Lawer

"A man's heart plans his way,
But the LORD directs his steps."
Proverbs 16:9 (NKJV)

I remember as a young girl thinking about the direction I wanted my life to go. I thought about going to college and graduating with a bachelor's degree and becoming a registered nurse by the age of twenty-two or twenty-three, meeting the love of my life, getting married by the age of twenty-five, hopefully having my first child by the age of twenty-seven, my second (and probably last) child by the age of thirty. Sounds like a fairy tale, right? I thought so too, but none of those things I planned in my head happened the way I had hoped.

Before having a real, genuine relationship with God, I thought about my life and how it is was my own. Little did I know back then that my plans are not God's plans. I never even thought about what God wanted for my life. I was selfish in my thinking. But as my walk and relationship with God grew stronger, the ideas of how I felt my life should be quickly changed.

I did not go to college right after graduating high school. So that right there proves I started out in the wrong direction for what I had planned in my head for my future. I did attend Roper School of Nursing to see if the medical field was what I really wanted to work in. I graduated with my nursing assistant certificate and worked a couple of private sitting caregiver jobs right after graduating, but nothing permanent. I had a lot of freedom at that time and was in heavy party mode. I also worked at a couple of day cares at that time to make some extra money, but I wasn't making a whole lot of money.

About two years later, I got hired as a dispatcher for the Mount Pleasant Police Department and had what I believed was a good paying job with good benefits at that time and thought I had it made. I got my own apartment and thought, "Wow, at twenty years of age, I have it going on." I ended up getting pregnant out of wedlock at the age of twenty but had a miscarriage in my fourth month of pregnancy.

My baby's father and I did not stay together. At first, my heart was crushed. Not because of the breakup, though. I got excited about becoming a mother and then I would get sad and depressed every time I saw another pregnant woman walking by me. I was jealous of that other woman and questioned God about why He didn't allow me to carry my baby to full term. Then I realized that was not in God's plan or at least not in His timing that He wanted it to happen for me. I also came to the realization that I wasn't ready to become a mother at that time and God knew that, and He was saving me from what probably would have been a lot of trials and tribulations for me at that time.

Life went on from there, and after I turned twenty-five, I decided to change directions in how my life was going. I wanted a real career that I would enjoy and not just a job. I've always had an interest in the medical field, but being a nursing assistant wasn't what I really wanted to do because from being in that program and getting the training I received, I realized nursing assistants were overworked, underpaid, mistreated, and disrespected. I just knew I wouldn't be happy working under those type of circumstances.

At the end of 2002, I decided to go back to school where I studied medical assisting at a technical college in Charleston, the city where I lived. I obtained my associate of applied science degree. I found medical assisting to be very rewarding because I would be able to work in the medical field but not be limited to doing one thing. There are vast opportunities for medical assistants.

Just months before completing my program, I got pregnant again. So, here I was again, unwed and pregnant from a man who did not stick around. I was so ill during that pregnancy that I had to drop out of school and move back in with my mother. After giving birth to my beautiful daughter, the real struggle began. I was a single mother trying to work full time, take care of my daughter, and pay the bills to the point of feeling like I was drowning.

That was the moment my relationship with God grew stronger because He was the only one who could help me through my struggles. Sure, I had a village of family and friends who helped me, but I still wasn't at peace with life. Could this really be what God wanted for my life? I decided once my daughter got a little older, I would finish what I had begun and complete my medical assisting program at the technical college. I re-enrolled at the end of 2006 and graduated with an associate of applied science degree in January 2007.

In 2008, I moved to Charlotte, N.C., where I'd always wanted to live. I felt like I needed a change of scenery. I admit, it was a selfish move at that time, and I did not consult God about the move. I really left because I wasn't happy with my living situation. At the time, my household consisted of five people in a two-bedroom house. It was a cramped living space. Sure, I could have just moved into my own place right here in Charleston, but like I said, I'd always wanted to experience living in Charlotte. At that time, apartments in Charlotte were less expensive than Charleston, and the pay was much better there. I still struggled financially, but for just a little while in Charlotte. At times, I felt a little depressed because I didn't have my village right there close to us when I needed help.

After two years of being in Charlotte, my mom fell ill from another stroke. This one had left her partially paralyzed on one side, and I moved back to Charleston to help care for her. So, here I was again, living in a cramped space. I also found out that my mom's home was in foreclosure and we would have to move out soon.

At this point, I kind of took control, or at least I thought I was in control. I found an apartment for us all to move into. While living there, of course, it was still cramped living, but it was better than the two-bedroom house we had been living in. My family and I started getting ourselves back on track financially. I was starting to be content in that area of my life, but in my personal life, not so much.

I never really had a real, meaningful relationship with anyone in the earlier parts of my adult life except for a guy I was seeing right after I graduated high school. We were on and off for a few years. My desire has always been to be married with a family of my own, but things didn't seem to work in my favor. I pretty much gave him an ultimatum that if he wasn't planning on marrying me, then I would leave. He did propose, but only because he didn't want to lose me and not because he wanted to make me his wife. We broke up two months before we had planned to get married. I felt frustrated at that point and felt that all men only wanted one thing and a lifetime commitment was not it.

From that point, it seemed I was getting into dead end "friends with benefits" situations and not relationships. I started blaming myself for not being good enough. I also realized I gave too much of myself in relationships when my status was just girlfriend and not wife. As the old saying goes: why buy the cow when you can get the milk for free? But then I thought maybe it wasn't God's plan for my life to be married.

This was when I said to myself, "I've had enough. I need to re-direct my direction in life." I had to stop selfishly thinking about what I wanted and going after what I wanted and start seeking God for guidance about what I needed, what He wanted for my life, and how He wanted me to approach it. I noticed that when I started to not concern myself with the things of the world and I focused more on how God wanted me to be as a human being and what He wanted for me, that's when I started having peace with where I was in my life and things appeared to be turning around.

Although I'm not quite where I imagined I would be in life or even where I want to be in life, I am far more ahead of where I thought I could be. I'm still taking care of my mother, who is a joy to care for, and my daughter, who is now a teenager and doing great academically and socially. I'm thankful and grateful that I'm not in any major debt. Our family of five still lives together in a three-bedroom apartment, but we have everything we need to survive.

Although things didn't go according to my timeline that I set, I know now that God had a better plan for me and all I needed to do was trust Him and believe that He would supply all my needs. When you want different results, you must do different things. You must focus and re-direct your thoughts and re-direct your actions. I stopped partying and stopped worrying what others thought of me. I started loving myself for who I was. I started praying and reading the Word of God for myself. In all things, good and bad, I give thanks to God, and now I live in peace, knowing where my help comes from.

Proverbs 3:5-6 (NKJV) states, *"Trust in the Lord with all your heart, / And do not lean on your own understanding. / In all your ways acknowledge Him, / And He shall direct your paths."* Now when I get a thought in my head or a feeling in my heart, whether good or bad, I stop and talk to God about it so that I don't make a move on my own that I may potentially regret later. I now seek God for direction in every aspect of life. I trust Him and believe He will never lead me down any path alone.

Psalm 32:8 (NKJV) states, *"I will instruct you and teach you in the way you should go; / I will guide you with My eye."* So, my prayer for anyone that's reading this is to always stay in relationship with God, seek Him for direction, and trust His guidance.

A Personalized Destination

Vera Brown

"The power of the tongue is life and death—

those who love to talk will eat what it produces" Proverbs 18:21

(ISV). Perhaps that's the reason our elders may have chastised a child

by saying, "Watch your mouth!"

Growing up in a very rural area in the '60s while the effects of

segregation were still very prevalent, I was always told, "You have to

know twice as much as them or you have to work twice as hard as

them." I didn't totally grasp the concept, but I understood that

mediocrity was not an option.

I also grew up in an era in which professional career choices

for women appeared to be limited to that of a nurse or a teacher,

neither of which I wanted to pursue. Since mediocrity was not an option, I recall responding to an inquiry of my career of interest by saying, "I want to be a counselor." Even as a teenager, I knew that I wanted to help others. And even though, like many teenagers, I had many painful distractions along the way, here I am today...

Distractions come in many forms, and for many teenagers, it may include looking for love in all the wrong places. Thank goodness through all of those prayer meetings I attended unwillingly as a teenager, a fear—no, reverence—for God was instilled in me, and I didn't stray too far away! Long story short, I entered college at seventeen years old only because it was expected; remember, mediocrity wasn't an option. An associate degree and low paying jobs set the tone for the need of more education. Ten years later (in 1983), after heartbreak and multiple mediocre jobs, I earned a bachelor's degree in—guess what? Guidance and counseling. It just sort of happened? Ahhh no! Remember what I said ... I wanted to be a counselor!

Fate would have it that I met a delightful little white woman in the '90s who shared my passion for grief counseling. As they used to say back in the day, talk brings on talk. As we talked, I learned that she not only knew my family on Old Pond Road, but she loved them. We bonded immediately! She invited me to grief sessions at a funeral home to get my feet wet in the field of grief counseling and to introduce me to someone considered to be a guru in the field—quite an honor it was!

Yep, I was on my way until fear crept in. Fear and insecurity stuck their ugly heads up and said, "You can't work with these people who don't look like you." And guess what—I bought into it. I abandoned ship and this woman that God had placed in my life. Feeling disappointed, regretful, and a sense of repentance, I was later given instructions in a dream: "When God opens a door, walk through." These are instructions that I've tried to be mindful of to this day!

Although grief counseling was my passion and my calling, I jumped ship! But God is faithful even when we aren't. I'm always reminded of Romans 8:28 (NIV): *"And we know that in all things God works for the good of those who love him, who have been called according to his purpose. "* When my mother died, it was then that I could without a doubt say I got it. I finally understood the NEED for grief counseling. It was then that I was propelled into my DESTINY, my purpose in professional counseling.

Remember that bachelor's degree in guidance and counseling obtained ten years after high school? Well, that led to a position as a special education teacher and later a position as a guidance counselor—yes, in that order. It was there that I recognized that children needed professional counseling to deal with trauma in their lives caused by deaths, murders, incarcerations, family dysfunction, and just life itself!

Mediocrity was still not an option, so I knew that I had work to do. I had to get ready, so back to graduate school I went. Not right away, though, because fear crept in and staged a roadblock once more.

You see, there were some requirements that were quite intimidating, and the enemy convinced me that I could not meet them. The enemy convinced me for years that I could not afford to go back to graduate school again, that I was too old, that I couldn't afford to work under a counseling supervisor for two years—where would I get the money from?

Most frightening of all, the enemy convinced me that there was no way I could pass the state's licensing exam! After all, some folks complained about having to take "that exam" three to four times! Fear is NOT of God, and I'm a witness! I truly believe that fear is a precursor of success and that fear comes in as a distraction from that which God has already ordained! Needless to say, all of the things I feared on the journey to licensure were conquered! Conquered to the point that my study partner and I met weekly, prayed, prepared, and passed the test on the first try! Conquered to the point that a counseling supervisor took me and my study partner under her wings and supervised us for FREE, while two other supervisors provided services to us at group rates!

As I observed individuals and families, particularly in my community and in the church world, I realized my mission was two-fold. The stigma regarding mental health counseling needs to be broken. There's so much help available to families, available just for the asking. So, why is it that so often in the African American community there is a stigma that allows dysfunction and prevents us from receiving professional counseling? We suffer in silence with mental health issues such as anxiety, depression, adjustment disorders, personality disorders, substance abuse, and many other conditions needlessly.

Proverbs 11:14 (ESV) says, *"Where there is no guidance, a people falls, / but in an abundance of counselors there is safety."* Culturally and traditionally, we have come to believe that seeing a counselor or therapist implies a lack of faith or is a sign of weakness, both of which are far from the truth. God in His infinite wisdom has empowered doctors, lawyers, counselors, and others to meet every need in our lives. He can provide our needs supernaturally or He can use whoever He has destined.

Remember what I said ... I wanted to be a counselor! Destiny would have it that the stage was set, doors were opened, and in obedience, I walked through the door to become a licensed professional counselor and the door to become a certified grief counselor. Here I am today, delayed but not denied. Go ahead and call those things that are not as though they were, as Romans 4:17 says, and just wait and see what happens!

Dismiss those thoughts that say, "You can't do it because ..." Remember Romans 8:31 (NIV): *"If God is for us, who can be against us?"*

Blessings!

Be Encouraged

Diane E. Green

"'Behold, God is my salvation;
I will trust, and will not be afraid;
for the LORD GOD is my strength and my song,
he has become my salvation.'"
Isaiah 12:2 (ESV)

In my daily prayers each day, I ask for God to allow my smile to brighten someone's day. I keep the thought of making others happy in my heart as I continue my assignment. I give words of encouragement and smiles to all whom I encounter.

As I rise early each morning and give thanks and praises to my God for another day, I look forward to walking through those doors of my God-ordained assignment, with whoever or wherever God sends me. Although I was hesitant at first to accept the call of encouragement because of being comfortable in the flesh, God started talking to me and through my peers, sending confirmation to me that this is where He needs me.

Fasting and praying has taught me not to question God's commands based off "wants" and being comfortable in the flesh. I was more comfortable in everything else but trusting in God's promises for my life. The Father knows exactly what our purpose is before we do. In Jeremiah 29:11, the Word of God tells us, *"'For I know the plans I have for you,' declares the LORD, 'plans to prosper you and not to harm you, plans to give you hope and a future'"* (NIV).

We need to learn to trust God no matter what it looks like. God tells us in His Word to *"trust in the Lord with all thine heart; and lean not unto thine own understanding"* (Proverbs 3:5 KJV). So why do we continue questioning God's command for our lives when given an assignment? Like I already said, I have learned to trust God in the commands and assignments He sends my way.

When I first started this assignment, which is my current job, I was offered a position based off my smile and my pleasant personality. Since being here for almost two years, I have met many new people! Some come and some go, but being on assignment, I am sure to leave them with a word from God and try to instill the Lord's Word into all I meet. Many ask, "Why are you always happy?" Others ask, "Where do you get these encouraging words from?" I explain to all of them that when one is obedient to God and lives in His glory, it flows from God through you!

On many occasions, I have given encouraging words to my co-workers, but in one special conversation recently, I felt encouraged to move in the Spirit. I had a conversation with one of my co-workers over lunch, and it was like God was talking through her to me. She enlightened me on how I have made her and others' faith in God stronger over the course of me working there. She also continued to say that I should expand and advance and share my spirit with more people. God has spoken once again, and this assignment is now coming to an end.

As you travel through your daily journey, give a smile to someone as you pass them by so that you know your living shall not be in vain! My God said, "Encourage my people! Give them comfort!" I know that I am more than a conqueror, for God lives in me and I will not stop encouraging others until that moment I take my last breath! God's will is for me to bring His kingdom here on earth!

I challenge every one of you each day as you encounter others to give them a smile, encourage them with a word. For example, "You look nice today," or "What a beautiful day that the Lord has made today!" Say something that may change someone's thinking or their attitude. It could have very well been very negative! Let others know that they can conquer anything that they put their minds to do.

"I will bless the Lord at all times: his praise shall continually be in my mouth" (Psalms 34:1 KJV). Never give up on yourself or others because God never gave up on us! We are all conquerors who

Damaged but Not Destroyed

Andrea Johnson-Weathers

I grew up in the biggest home in my neighborhood. I shared

this home with my beautiful mother, father, and siblings. Everyone

considered me "rich" because of how things appeared. My dad was a

merchant seaman, and because of his job, he would be gone for

months at a time, leaving my mother to take care of me and my

siblings.

I kept a smile on my face, but I was miserable. I would go to

school on an empty stomach, and at lunch I would stay in class

because I was embarrassed that I didn't have anything to eat. This

lasted until I finished elementary school. My dad started to come

home more frequently on the weekends, but he also started drinking

more. My dad started cheating on my mother, and they began to have verbal arguments, which led into physical altercations. My siblings and I hated to watch them fight. But I felt the need to protect my mother. Things would get so bad that my mother and I would hide in her closet behind her clothes until my father fell asleep. This went on for years and years.

The emotional trauma didn't stop there. At the age of 12, I was molested by one of my older brothers. He would come into my room late at night while everyone was asleep. I would lie on my side and pretend I was asleep. I was afraid to tell anyone. Sadly, the abuse didn't stop there. Another one of my brothers would put me behind a wooden stove and make me stand there for hours while my mother wasn't home. The heat was so severe I couldn't move if I wanted to. I still have the burn marks to prove it.

I always asked God why He put me in such an abusive family. I was the youngest out of all and was left to defend myself and protect my mother. "*'For I know the plans I have for you,' declares the Lord, 'plans to prosper you and not to harm you, plans to give you hope and a future'*" (Jeremiah 29:11 NIV).

I became a damaged child. I was intimidated and started to get anxiety as I entered high school. I would try to avoid going home so I joined the track team and entered into different after-school activities. Through all this, I still kept a smile in public. You never know what others go through, and you can't judge a book by its cover! *"Walk by faith and not by sight"* (2 Corinthians 5:7 NKJV). My parents stopped supporting me financially, so I had to get a summer job. I bought my own clothing and all the necessities that I needed.

I never had the intention of going to college. I figured after high school I could've found a decent job to support myself. But in reality, I wanted to escape my childhood. So, I applied for college. My first year in college was good but lonely. I would find myself coming home a lot on the weekend to visit my boyfriend at the time. By my sophomore year in college, I was pregnant. When my father got the news that I was expecting, he told me, "You aren't worth nothing and never will be." I carried that thought with me throughout most of my adulthood, and I promised myself I would never marry someone like my dad. I attended college up until my junior year. I dropped out and decided to give all my dedication to my child.

Twelve years later, and I had three more kids for a man I met while working together. Sadly, this man had the exact same personality as my dad. The relationship was horrible, but I was blessed with my kids. This man would have infidelities with many different women. It caused me so much pain. I couldn't believe history was repeating itself. I was living in a generational curse. I knew what the right thing to do was. I knew that I deserved better, so one day, I found the courage to leave him.

After I left my children's father, one morning around 3 a.m. as I lay next to my children in bed, I jumped up to notice a man. He had jumped the window and molested me right there. The sad part is that I knew exactly who he was. My kids were too young to witness or remember such a thing, so I cried silently as he raped me. After he left, I got up and put a knife in each window so that he wouldn't be able to enter my house again. I was ashamed and felt dirty.

Around this time, I started to believe my father's words. I wasn't worth nothing and never would be. I didn't understand why I had to go through all this and endure so much pain.

After going through such hard times, I finally felt a sense of relief. I had met a man who became my best friend. After dating for a while, we got married. I thought the relationship was real, almost perfect, for twelve years. Until one day I got a call from a man saying that my husband and his wife were having an affair. For a while, it was hard to believe. But many other things happened, and we got divorced.

God shook up my world just to show me that He is first. Pain has a way of making you call on God and humbling you. At the end of the day, He is all that we have. He is my father, so I asked to be healed and He healed me. I learned that no man should be placed above Him. "*In all your ways submit to him, / and he will make your paths straight*" (Proverbs 3:6 NIV). With God, there's always an appointed time for everything, and when you put Him first, trust His timing, and keep the faith, blessings will come down! You can't believe in dreams if you don't believe in the giver of your dreams.

I am more than a conqueror because God spared me even though I placed people before Him. He forgave me, and in return, I forgave myself. Thank you, God, for never leaving me! I found God throughout my struggle. If I never went through these things, I wouldn't know how to call on Him.

Do you take time to read the Bible? Do you know there are dark places as well as the Holy Spirit? The dark side is called witchcraft, which preys on you before you are even born. I believe that everyone that caused me pain did it because someone had caused them pain prior. Therefore, it's about knowing how to pray and knowing how to war against the dark side and break generational curses. Be true to yourself!

The Power of Unity

Fredricka Terry

"Finally, all of you, have unity of mind, sympathy, brotherly love, a tender heart, and a humble mind." 1 Peter 3:8 (ESV)

"We've learned to fly the air like birds, we've learned to swim the seas like fish. And yet we haven't learned to walk the earth as brothers and sisters."
— Rev. Dr. Martin Luther King Jr.

The importance of unity is something I had to learn. Whether it is unity within a family, friends, church, or a small group, just like the verse from 1 Peter 3:8 reminds us, unity is a choice. It's a decision that goes beyond one of us and benefits all of us. I had to come to terms with this more than once in my life. Now, however, I understand that not one of us is an island, meant to live this life alone and separated. We need the support of others, and we need to learn to support them as well.

From the beginning, I remember how hard it was to be raised away from my sisters and brothers. When I was two years old, my mother passed away. There were many children in the home, so I, as the youngest, was sent to live with my aunt. I would visit in the summertime and go back up north when school started. After my grandmother's death, I was packed up and sent to Charleston to live with my eldest sister. The adjustment for me was hard. Don't be mistaken, though. I've lived a beautiful life, full of love and laughter and good relationships. I am thankful to God Almighty for every day that He gives me. However, there has also been some hardship, some pain, and some tragedy.

At this time, I was about to enter middle school. My siblings had grown up with one another, so I often found myself trying to fit in, learn from them, and even just have a relationship. We would always have Thanksgiving and Christmas together, which was so much fun. My brothers came into town, and we would all gather as a family. That was when I felt the most loved and like I was a part of my family. That was when I felt the unity.

As I got older, however, everyone started to live their own lives. Feelings started to change. I'd had a child out of wedlock and later experienced a failed relationship. There was no one for me to talk to anymore because now I was judged. Therefore, I mostly kept to myself. My support system had moved away, so I was alone with my son.

This is when I would have to discover unity and strength through my faith. I eventually found guidance through gospel music, specifically Mary Mary's song "Can't Give Up Now." I would allow the words to wash over me, and despite the up and down or the back and forth I was experiencing, I felt connected to something greater than myself. I didn't feel so alone. Eventually, since I was out of state at the time, I moved back to Charleston.

I was living my life, just going through the motions until the devil tried to attack me in full force by going against my son. *I did not know what to do.* He faced a situation that had the potential to affect the rest of his life. His reputation was on the line and possibly his future. I didn't know where to start. All of a sudden, right was left, and up was down. The only thing I knew was that my child needed me, and it seemed like I was all he had.

Our entire family knew the situation and what was going on in our home. In the beginning, I believed that we would all be there for one another, but that assumption quickly changed. That crushing feeling of being alone returned in full force. In the wake of this hardship, sides were chosen, and I, oftentimes, had to stand by myself. Eventually, nights of drinking and crying would slip me into a depression.

Of course, I was praying and praying. I asked God what to do. Why was this happening? What did I do wrong in my son's life? Then, one day, I got a phone call from a nephew about my son, saying, "Fred, go get him. He does not belong there." The next day, my sister called and told me to come to her home. My brother had sent us all a love gift, and she was giving her part to me to help. Not long afterwards, I also got a call from a friend, *of another faith*, who came to my home and had Bible study with me, so that I would be encouraged by the Word of God and not lose hope.

Understand this: Tragedy, big or small, hits every person differently. The aftermath of grief or suffering and how they affect our lives are as unique to each of us as the hair on our heads or fingerprints on our hands. They are similar, but different. I, personally, know my fair share of hardship. This was a hard time in my life. Thankfully, as I have learned, God is still there in the dark.

According to the Bible, God says, *"Don't panic. I'm with you. / There's no need to fear for I'm your God. / I'll give you strength. I'll help you. / I'll hold you steady, keep a firm grip on you"* (Isaiah 41:10 MSG). When I was at the lowest point, the Lord reached down and held me firm by sending others to stand with me and help hold me up. He pulled me out of darkness into His marvelous light (1 Peter 2:9). By the Lord's grace, the situation with my son was resolved, and we've been able to move forward with our lives. However, to my surprise, it was not through great miracles or supernatural acts of wonder that my faith was restored. It was through simple, yet overt, acts of kindness. It was from unexpected phone calls or notes. It was from gifts of love. God working through people helped me believe and have faith again. It was slow at first for me, but it has been a journey, and I now understand something important. Unity. U-N-I-T-Y. It is such a simple, yet powerful, word, and it changed everything for me.

So, every day when I wake up, I pray to God. I ask for many things: my son's and family's well-being, peace at my job, and His hands on the world around me amongst other things. But I promise that I NEVER ask, "How can I make somebody else's life miserable today?" That has never been my goal. As a matter of fact, my desire is quite the opposite. My goal is to bless others as I have been blessed.

Something I'm known for amongst my friends and family is a longstanding vision of the future that I've held for years: One day, when my time here is done, I will go to the other side. There, I'll see Peter at those pearly gates, and he'll ask me if, while I was on earth, I did my best. And I'll answer without a shred of hesitation, "I did all I could." I did all I could to help somebody I saw in need—no matter their age or what they looked like. I did all I could to leave positivity wherever I went and not tolerate negative or evil acts. I did all I could do to live a life that was full—of hope, of smiles, of laughter, and of joy. I did all that I could to live a life that was pleasing to the Lord.

My dream and my goal is and has always been to live life without regret, to know that I did all I could to help others and to be an example through my actions and deeds of the power of unity and oneness. I believe that it is up to each of us to go after the life we want—together—and to do our best to encourage others to do the same.

Seasons and Life Events

Shirley Young Doctor

"To everything there is a season, / A time for every purpose under heaven" (Ecclesiastes 3:1 NKJV). Recognize the season you are in. Accept where you are and use it to your advantage. Discover the blessings in your present season and treasure them. Take the successes and wisdom from past seasons and bring them to your present one. Leave the failures of the past behind. Most important of all, as you walk through this season and ones to come, remember: He has made everything beautiful in His time (Ecclesiastes 3:11).

I grew up in a family of ten siblings. One died during childbirth, but I was the sixth child. I knew nothing about love growing up. My mother and father argued and fought every day of my life until he passed. I was twenty- one when that happened. My siblings grew up and left home with the exception of my two younger brothers and myself. I was eighteen when I got pregnant with my son in January 1975. I graduated in June of that same year from high school and got married in December 1975.

I didn't know anything about the personal issues of life. As I grew up in life, sex was a forbidden subject in my household. All I knew was my mother said, "Girls should keep their dress down." Growing up, I didn't know what that meant. I started liking my neighborhood boy down the street from me. We played together like every normal child would, and then he began to have interest in me. This is when I learned about what sex was, in May 1974. I went home, and immediately my brother picked up that something was wrong or different with me. We talked about it, and he was very angry and said we had to get married, so we did.

In my mind, I knew this was not what I wanted and he was not the man for me, but I was ashamed of what I did and I'd already embarrassed my mom, so this was the right thing for me to do. I was still a teenager, and I didn't have a life, so I was angry because I saw my other friends hanging out and enjoying life. I wanted to be like them, and I was thinking, "I didn't ask for this." But I knew I had to be accountable for my actions. We got divorced in 1977 and have stayed great friends to this day.

In August of 2000, I got married again, and with this marriage there were no children. My other two children were from previous relationships. My husband was a minister or so I thought that he was. I met him and within six months, we were married. Once again, I was searching for love in all the wrong places and trying to please my mom at the same time, thinking that she would see the good in me.

Everything was going well with the exception of if you weren't in the Holiness religion, then you couldn't be my friend. I allowed him to isolate me from my family and friends. I wasn't allowed to see my friends or my family like I wanted to, but I could be with his family only. As years began to pass by, I began to see signs of something that disturbed me that would lead to someone spending some time in jail. I apologized to God and asked Him to release me from this marriage. We divorced in June 2006. I left his home and moved back with my mom with my two children because the oldest was in the military.

I moved back home with my mother with my two girls, and this was when my season of life began to shift. This was when I really found out that I was the black sheep. I moved back home, and I thought I was literally in HELL. My mom was a minister or so I thought that's who she was. Once again, I was looking for love. My girls were terrified of her, and my younger daughter kept asking me, "Is she your real mom?" My children and I were treated so bad. My kids would go to school and stay at the neighbor's house until I got home from work because they didn't want to be there alone.

We were confined in one bedroom, and it was a three-bedroom house. She would search through my mail and go through my personal things when I wasn't at home. I could tell because I would place things in a particular way, and when I got back, it was not how I left things. My daughters and I would be talking and laughing in our room with the door closed, and she would just come in and say, "Oh y'all talking and laughing at me." My kids and I looked dumfounded, like, "No ma'am." So many things went on that I don't want to discuss that weren't right.

I told my older siblings, and some agreed but two said, "Impossible. She would not say or do things like that." They weren't staying there; we were. We started leaving home early in the morning and weekends and didn't come back until bedtime. I believed this made her very angry because she started accusing me of things.

The first time I ever talked back to my mother in my entire life was when we came in from dinner and she said to me, "God told me that you came here to take over my house." Say what, wait a minute, Momma, are you serious? So, I chuckled in unbelief. She went and got a wooden baseball bat and raised it to hit me.

I looked at her and said, "Well, you might as well hit me because I am not going to hit you back." She kept on arguing and I just looked at her. She finally left the room and went in the living room, and I could hear her talking. She called this nosey lady down the street and told her that I wanted to fight her. That was far from the truth.

Still, I was trying to let her see the good in me because I had two failed marriages and two kids out of wedlock, and she looked down on me because of that. My kids were terrified and wanted to know why she treated me like that. That's the way she always treated me unless she wanted something. I came to realize that no matter how hard I tried, nothing I did would've pleased her, though she bragged on a few of her other children. I decided that I needed to get my kids out of this toxic environment.

I had been living there for free. I found an apartment and we left, and that was the best decision I ever made. We had a peace that surpasses all understanding (Philippians 4:7). My headaches and stress were lifted. It was so hard for me to call and talk to her after I left because of what I went through as a mother and daughter. I had grown in the Lord so much by then, and I continued to pray and ask God to help me to call her just to say hi. I was grown, in my thirties, and I would pick up the phone to call her and would get scared and hang up. I knew that what we had as a mother and daughter relationship was lost, but I wanted so badly just for her to accept me as her child, to love me unconditionally. A mother's love is so precious to a daughter. I have friends that when I saw their mothers love on them and kiss them, I would cry. I wanted a mom that I could never have.

I finally got to the point where I would call and not hang up, but our conversation was so short. She would in turn call from time to time to check on us. We never developed a mother to daughter relationship. She passed away four years ago, and that was the worst day of my life because she didn't get to be my mother. At that moment, oh how I wished that my seasons would start all over again with the perfect mom.

All the love and energy that I had for my mother I put in my children. I felt that I could move on and be happy after she died. I am no longer that same person who was in and out of relationships because I thought my mother wouldn't approve. Yes, I was grown and still feared her because that's all I knew. My children know for a fact that I love them. I not only tell them, but I showed them and still do. My grandchildren are my heart, and I shower them with love. I tell them every day that they are smart, handsome, beautiful, and wonderfully made. I love them and they are my gems.

In my new season, I am blessed and know it. When I reflect over the years in my life that I've gone through, I knew God was there. He was preparing me for a day when I would realize my worth and the purpose of why He made me. I've been transformed into a victorious and phenomenal woman of God. My trust issue and doubts about myself are completely gone. I was once a broken vessel, but now I am a child of the most high God and I can soar like an eagle. I have no worries because I am an overcomer and a conqueror. I lie safe in the bosom of God.

I am believing that my change has finally come, and my season has shifted. *"To everything there is a season, / A time for every purpose under heaven"* (Ecclesiastes 3:1 NKJV). Recognize the season you're in. Accept where you are and use it to your advantage. Discover the blessings in your present season and treasure them. Take the successes and wisdom from your past seasons and bring them into your present one. Leave the failure of the past behind. Most important of all, as I walk through this season and the ones to come, I must remember: *"He has made everything beautiful in its time"* (Ecclesiastes 3:11 NKJV).

Renewal of Faith

Mable Terry Washington

Matthew 5:3 states that, *"'Blessed are the poor in spirit, / For theirs is the kingdom of heaven'"* (NKJV). This verse is from the Beatitudes of Jesus and is part of the Sermon on the Mount that Jesus spoke. Each beatitude speaks to a characteristic in one's life and discusses how Christians are blessed through their faith in God. When I read this verse, I am reminded of a time when nothing seemed to be going right in my life and I had lost my faith.

As a child, I was raised as a Christian and I grew up going to church with my family. My faith was important to me; however, as a young, single mother, I was struggling to make ends meet. I questioned why God would allow me to struggle in this way, so I had stopped praying. With two young daughters at home depending on me, I found myself in survival mode. Each month, I found myself in a position where I had enough money to pay our rent but would then

79

have to make the decision to buy food or to pay our utility bills. It was difficult understanding during those times while struggling how 1 Thessalonians 5:18 (ESV)—*"Give thanks in all circumstances; for this is the will of God in Christ Jesus for you"*—was God's will for me.

As a parent, you want to be the best that you can be for your children and give them all the things they need and that their hearts desire. You dream of giving them the things you didn't have as a child, hoping one day it will come true.

One Christmas, my daughters were five and six years old. They didn't ask for a lot of toys or clothes, but they were begging me to put up a Christmas tree. I wanted to give them a magical Christmas with everything that they wanted, but I knew that if I put up a Christmas tree that would be all that we would have. There was simply no money for gifts to go under the tree. Still, I decided to put up our tree and get into the holiday spirit as much as I could. One evening, after buying my girls something to eat, I was able to go to a drug store and purchase them one gift each. I found them board games on sale, and I put the gifts under the tree for Christmas morning.

That Christmas morning, one of my girls' friends stopped by to see what they received for Christmas. She came in and looked around and said to my girls, "Oh ... that's all y'all got?" My five-year-old stepped up and said to her, "Christmas is only one day a year, but my mama does for us all of the time."

Her words struck me as being so powerful, and they made me so proud to be her mother. While I was focused on not being able to provide what I thought I should or what society was telling me that they needed, it turned out that what I provided for them on a daily basis—my heart, my love—was enough for her.

First Peter 5:6-7 says, *"Humble yourselves therefore, under God's mighty hand, that he may lift up in due time. Cast all your anxiety on him because he cares for you"* (NIV).

I wish I could say that I was immediately humbled from that one experience and that I was returned to my faith, but it took a little longer for me to get to that place. It wasn't long after that Christmas that I found myself looking for a job. I ran into a friend one day and mentioned that I was on the hunt for new employment. She told me that I should go to the hospital and put in an application.

Right away, I walked to the hospital and inquired about open positions. The lady at the desk told me that she was sorry, but that they didn't have any openings in environmental services. Her comment made me look up so fast that I almost gave myself whiplash! I told her that I didn't have anything against environmental services, but that I was not interested in that department. I asked if there was anything available for a clerical position, and it turned out that there were some openings. That day, I filled out an application, and she actually asked me if I wanted to go ahead and interview for the position on the spot. What? Now?! I told her that I wasn't dressed appropriately, but that I would love to come back and interview when I was more presentable. Somehow, she convinced me that I was fine and that I should speak to the hiring supervisor on that day.

When I went in for the interview, I swear we talked about everything EXCEPT the job! We talked about our families, the flowers in her office, and our life experiences. The job never really came up, but at the end of our talk, she asked me when I could start. I told her that I could start today! We laughed and settled on me starting on Monday. I worked there at the hospital for forty-two very happy years.

While working there, my position changed several times over the years. I worked my way up through the ranks, and I thoroughly enjoyed my job for all of those years. It was during my time working for the hospital that I humbled myself and returned to my faith. I realized that everything that had worked out for me happened in God's timing and not my own. The job that I wanted did not come to me when I wanted it, but when God decided it was the right time to present me with the opportunity.

It bothered me for years that I was not able to complete my degree at Benedict College when I wanted to because I had to return home. But in God's timing, I was able to finish my degree and even received my bachelor's degree from Strayer University in 2010 with a of GPA 4.0 at the age of 62 years old.

Matthew 7:7-8 says, *"Ask, and it shall be given you; seek, and ye shall find; knock, and it shall be opened unto you. For everyone that asketh receiveth, and he that seeketh findth; and to him that knocketh it shall be opened"* (KJV). I want to leave you with two lessons I have come to realize during the many storms of life:

Lesson 1: Everyone has a season of what some call trials and tribulations. I realize that I'm never alone; God always has my back, no matter the size of the storm.

Lesson 2: Be thankful for everything, big and small, non-materialistic and material. Be thankful and grateful for all things.

Throughout the years, I have learned a lot. My faith is stronger, and God is first in whatever I do. God is my lifeline, and in everything, I give thanks.

About the Authors

First Lady Janet Snipe has served alongside her

husband Pastor William Snipe as First Lady for many years and they reside in Goose Creek, SC. She's the mother of two wonderful children, Apostle DoQuoi T. Green (Pastor Donna P. Green), and D'Leta K. Snipe-Waring (Dezmond Waring). She's the grandmother of three beautiful grandchildren, London, D'Laysia, and Alathia. Janet has earned a Bachelor of Science degree in Business Management and a Master's Degree in Health Services Administration. She has retired after serving 30 years at MUSC Hospital. Janet is the Founder of the Fervent Ladies Christian book club ministry. She is now the Visionary Author of "We Are More Than Conquerors," the Co-Author of Amazon's Best Seller "No More Residue" and the Co-Author of "Overcoming Adversity: Pushing Past the Pain". Janet has a great love for people and a passion to help others accomplish all God has placed in them. Janet's loving nature, generosity and gift of wisdom has afforded her the distinct privilege to consult many individuals from diverse backgrounds and professions.

For more info please visit www.janetgsnipe.com

Email: j-snipe@hotmail.com

Cassandra Middleton Minson was born on

December 6, 1956 in Charleston, SC. A native of Johns Island, SC, Cassandra is dedicated to lending a helping hand and spreading her love for life with everyone.

A retired educator of thirty-four years with the Charleston County School District, Cassandra believes that all children have their own unique way of learning. Cassandra received her bachelor of arts degree in liberal arts from Morris College, Sumter, SC, and a master of arts degree in early childhood education from Walden University in Minneapolis, MN.

Cassandra strives daily to follow the words of Proverbs 16:3. It's a lesson that she and her husband, Leroy Minson, instilled in their three children—Lakeleia (Sheldon), Meagan (Markevais), and Rashida—at an early age. A hallmark to Cassandra's legacy are her four handsome grandsons: Deontaye, Jeremiah, Carson, and Braxton.

At a young age, Cassandra's mother, the late Mary Middleton Pinckney noticed her daughter's passion for playing the piano and encouraged her to take piano lessons. Within two years, Cassandra learned the basic techniques and God made her vision clear by anointing her hands while strengthening her with the gift to read music as well as play by ear. Cassandra continues to speak life through music at her church, where she has served as the minister of music for more than forty years.

Email: minsoncas@yahoo.com

D'Leta Snipe-Waring is the daughter of Rev.

William & First Lady Janet Snipe, the sister of Apostle DoQuoi Green, wife of Dezmond Waring, and mother of D'Laysia Waring.

D'Leta grew up in Goose Creek, S.C., but now resides in Ladson, S.C., with her family. She graduated from Stratford High School and Francis Marion University, earning a bachelor's degree in biology. She later furthered her education by becoming a certified massage therapist through Trident Technical College.

D'Leta currently attends Mt. Olive AMEC where her father is the pastor. In addition, she is a member of Upper Room Kingdom where her brother is the founder and head pastor. She loves spending quality time with her family, shopping, and going out to eat. D'Leta is a fun-loving woman of God who continues to seek the Lord, for she knows that her strength comes from Him. She strives to be like Jesus Christ and to keep Him first in all things that she does.

Email: d_snipe90@yahoo.com

Dr. Lakeleia Middleton Robinson,

affectionately known as "Pumpkin," was born in Charleston, S.C., to Cassandra Middleton Minson (Leroy) and Fredrick Stroud.

A faithful and dedicated member of Ferry Field Missionary Baptist Church in Johns Island, S.C., Dr. Robinson serves in various ministries under the leadership of Pastor James R. Townes. She is a born-again believer exercising faith in her everyday life and circumstances.

As a believer in community outreach, her involvement with the Fervent Ladies Book Club has afforded her the opportunity to serve those in need, give back to the community, and discover a path to spiritual growth.

Dr. Robinson received her undergraduate degree in social work from South Carolina State University. She earned a master of arts degree in human resources from Webster University and a doctorate in healthcare administration from Capella University.

Dr. Robinson has been married to her biggest supporter and number one fan, Sheldon Robinson, for seventeen years. They are the proud parents of two sons, Deontaye and Jeremiah. Dr. Robinson enjoys spending time with her family, traveling, and utilizing her charismatic personality to reach others for Christ. Her favorite Scripture is *"I can do all things through Christ who strengthens me"* (Philippians 4:13 NKJV).

Email: robinsonlakeleia@gmail.com

Tameka C. Lawer, also known as Tammy, was born

August 30, 1975, and raised on Johns Island, S.C. She is the mother of a beautiful daughter named Jada. She's also a caregiver to her mother, Maggie L. Wright, who fell ill and became disabled because of several strokes. Along with being a single mother and caregiver, she also works full time as a patient referral specialist with Roper St. Francis Homecare. She received her associate of applied science degree in medical assisting in 2007 and has since held several positions working in the healthcare sector.

She's a member of Ferry Field Baptist Church, where she serves on the Combined Choir, Gadsden Gospelaires Ensemble, and on the Christian Relations Ministry. Tameka is spiritually gifted by God to care for and assist others wherever assistance is needed. She has accepted the calling on her life and is passionate about walking in her purpose of being a great assistant, serving others, as God has commanded us. Nothing excites Tammy more than pleasing God through serving others.

Email: TLawer@hotmail.com

Vera Brown is a licensed professional counselor, certified grief

counselor, retired teacher, retired school counselor, encourager, and caregiver, and most importantly whereas some are Grandma, GiGi, or MeMe she is LaLa.

Vera Brown has a natural gift for helping children and youth. However, she also has a finesse for working with children, adolescents, and adults dealing with grief and loss, ADHD, anxiety, depression, and adjustment disorders or stress-related conditions where one feels overwhelmed and has a hard time adjusting to a stressful event or change, just to name a few areas. Her work is more than a nine to five but is her passion and life's purpose.

In building relationships with students and their families, she recognized the need for mental health counseling in many of the youth. This was the catalyst that convinced Vera to pursue a second master's degree, this time in mental health counseling, in addition to her master's degree in education.

She's a firm believer that "you have to meet people where they are spiritually, emotionally, academically, and every other area of their being ... because broken crayons can still color."

Email: ladyvlb@yahoo.com

Diane Elaine Green was born on February 17, 1965, on

Johns Island, S.C., to the late Thelma L. Green. She is the fourth of seven children. She has one daughter, Brittany D'Laina Louise Green and one granddaughter Brielle Z'Amour Green-Cochran.

Diane accepted Jesus Christ at the early age of 11 and served as a missionary at Ferry Field Baptist Church on Johns Island, S.C. Diane is a Navy veteran and served her country for sixteen years. She was formerly employed with United Postal Services for twenty-five years and is currently still employed at Geodis USA, Inc., as an accounts payable clerk.

Diane's favorite Scripture is: *"Behold I stand at the door, and knock; if any man hear my voice, and open the door, I will come in to him, and will sup with him, and he with me"* (Revelation 3:20 KJV).

Email: dianegreen45@yahoo.com

Andrea Johnson-Weathers was born into the

world by Samuel and Evelina Johnson. Andrea is the second youngest child of ten children. She grew up in Wadmalaw Island, the deep country of Charleston County, South Carolina.

In 1978, Andrea graduated from St. John's High School. Immediately, she went to college in Raleigh, N.C. However, the birth of her oldest daughter put a pause on those plans. From there, she went in the food and beverage industry for twelve years before she birthed three more beautiful children. Her children pushed her to further her education to be an example to them, "If Mama can do it, you can too." Thirty years later she earned an associate's degree from Virginia College for medical assisting. That's why Andrea always says, "It's never too late."

Email: andreaweathers17@gmail.com

Fredricka Terry is a woman of faith as well as

determination. A Charleston, S.C., native, Fredricka is the youngest of ten and the mother of one son, a local Charleston business owner. She is also a local entrepreneur, an associate of LegalShield, and a supervisor at the Medical University of South Carolina.

Fredricka enjoys owning a business (and working in an environment) of service because her ultimate goal has always been to help people. She believes that if you can't help someone, at least you should not hurt them. When the obstacles and stumbling blocks of life come, Fredricka remembers the old hymn "It is Well with My Soul." If she could pass along any message to current and future generations, it would be: stand in your faith.

Email: fwt2erm@yahoo.com

Shirley Young Doctor is a mother of three children

and six grandchildren. She has been a pharmacy technician for the past forty years—of that, twenty years was with the Department of Veterans Affairs. She is a member of Kingdom Vision Christian Center and holds the position of a leader and Head Department of the Ushers. She is a born-again believer and active in the ministry.

Shirley has earned her associate degree in health care administration from the University of Phoenix. She resides in Goose Creek, SC.

Email: doctor.shirley@yahoo.com

Mable Terry Washington was born December 19,

1949, to Minnie and William Terry, both deceased. She is the mother of four daughters, Kra'Shawn, Kennise, Kimberly, and Kristen; and grandmother of nine: six boys and three girls. Mable is a graduate of the Charles A. Brown High School, class of 1967, and Strayer University, class of 2010. She loves reading, traveling, shopping, and spending time with her family. She worked for forty-two years in the medical field as a telemetry technician. For years, she facilitated the orientation of professionals who would become doctors, nurses, and nurse anesthetists. Some would stay; some would go to other hospitals; however, many would come back and thank her for her training.

Now that she has retired from work, Mable is a community volunteer. She assists with the Tywanza Sanders entrepreneurial camp. Currently, she is in search of what the next phase of her life will hold. But whatever it is, she knows that it will involve helping and being a blessing to others. The verse Mable seeks to live by the most says, *"Whoever is generous to the poor lends to the LORD, / and he will repay him for his deed"* (Proverbs 19:17 ESV).

Email: mablew60@gmail.com

Works Cited

Alabama Gurlz. "Heaven Belongs to You." Track 10 on *"The Gurlz"
Live*, 4 Winds Records, 2014.

Logan, Cally. "What is Fervent Prayer and How Do We Do It?" June
19, 2019. Crosswalk.com. https://www.crosswalk.com/faith/prayer/
what-is-fervent-prayer.html

Mary, Mary. "Can't Give Up Now." Track 5 on *Thankful*, Columbia,
2000.

Turner, Norris. "They Call Me Crazy." HSH Records, 1968.

Made in the USA
Columbia, SC
28 April 2021